IDEA WISE

Porches & Sunrooms

*Inspiration & Information
for the Do-It-Yourselfer*

Jerri Farris

D0556584

Creative Publishing
international

CHANHASSEN, MINNESOTA
www.creativepub.com

Creative Publishing international

Copyright © 2006
Creative Publishing international, Inc.
18705 Lake Drive East
Chanhassen, Minnesota 55317
1-800-328-3895
www.creativepub.com

Printed in China

10 9 8 7 6 5 4 3 2 1

President/CEO: Ken Fund
Vice President/Publisher: Linda Ball
Vice President/Retail Sales & Marketing: Kevin Haas

Executive Editor: Bryan Trandem
Creative Director: Tim Himsel
Managing Editor: Tracy Stanley

Author: Jerri Farris
Editor: Thomas Lemmer
Senior Art Director: Dave Schelitzche
Photo Editor: Julie Caruso
Book Designer: Kristine Mudd
Technical Illustrator: Earl Slack
Production Manager: Laura Hokkanen
Proofreader: Sid Korpi

IdeaWise: Porches & Sunrooms

Library of Congress Cataloging-in-Publication Data

Farris, Jerri.
  Ideawise--porches & sunrooms :
inspiration & information for the
do-it-yourselfer / Jerri Farris.
     p. cm.
  ISBN 1-58923-223-2 (soft cover)
1. Porches--Design and construction--Amateurs' manuals. 2.
Sunspaces--Design and construction--Amateurs' manuals. 3.
Do-it-yourself work. I. Title: Porches & sunrooms. II. Title.
  TH4970.F375 2006
  747.7--dc22
                              2005017724

Table of Contents

Introduction

Porches—breezy, cozy, convivial spaces—are making a comeback. Not coincidentally, so are the arts of conversation, relaxation, and neighborhood connections. Homebuilders' organizations report that today's consumers are attracted to porches of every stripe—open, enclosed, front, side, back. Virtually every size, shape, and description of porch is appealing to a population searching for places to retreat from the frenetic pace of life, quiet spaces to share with family and friends, and opportunities to connect with nature.

Why are porches making a comeback? And how did they fall from favor in the first place? To answer these questions, we need to take a brief look at the history of the porch.

North Americans can trace the development of their porches to a wide variety of influences, among them ancient Greece and Rome, as well as 19th-century West Africa, India, Italy, and Spain. The many words used to refer to porches—veranda, piazza, gallery, terrace, lanai—reflect the diversity of these influences.

Like most developments in home building, early porches were a solution to a set of problems, chiefly heat and bugs. Knowing that it's often 15–20° F cooler in the shade than in direct sun, home builders began shading front entrances with the roofed structures that were the forbearers of the porch. Eventually, they found that raising a house off the ground provided better access to cooling breezes and discouraged insects to boot. The combination proved irresistible.

The first North American house known to have been built with a gallery, or porch, was constructed in Mobile, Alabama in 1702. By the mid 1800s, porches were common on homes for the well-to-do, particularly in the South. About that time, a new construction technique known as balloon framing entered the scene. In balloon-framed houses, a skeleton of lighter-weight lumber replaced the heavy timber frames of earlier times, making houses—and porches—easier and much less expensive to build. Within a few years, porches sprouted on homes across the economic spectrum.

For decades, porches were an integral part of family life. After the day's work was done, families gathered on the porch to enjoy one another's company and whatever cool breezes were available. Neighbors shared refreshments and news of the day.

This pattern continued until technological advances once again changed the patterns of family life. Cars, with their noise and smells and garages, intruded on the front yards; air conditioning made interior spaces more comfortable. The rising cost of land and the changing shape of lots also contributed to the demise of the porch: narrow lots didn't easily accommodate side or wrap-around porches.

By the mid-20th century, new homes rarely included porches. In fact, to some people, a porch signified that a house was old-fashioned and out-of-date, and thousands were torn down or allowed to fall into disrepair. Decks and patios drew families to the relative privacy of back yards, and neighbors withdrew from the easy patterns of communication that had marked the front-porch years.

That brings us to the end of the 20th century, when porches began their comeback. A number of factors have played into their resurgence: awareness of the dangers of direct sun exposure, an urge to reconnect with neighbors, and the nostalgia of baby boomers for the "good old days."

Today, entire communities are being developed around not just the physical structure of porches but around the *idea* of them. In Seascape, Florida; Apple Valley, Minnesota; and Portland, Oregon, to name a few, neighborhood covenants are consigning garages to the sides and backs of houses while sidewalks, front porches, and neighborhood gathering spaces are taking center stage.

If you're one of the millions of homeowners dreaming of a porch, this book is for you. Before we begin our exploration of porches, let's take a quick look at sunrooms.

Sunrooms have a history similar to that of porches but quite a different provenance. Glass structures used as greenhouses trace their roots all the way back to the Roman era, but modern sunrooms are more directly related to the English conservatories.

During the late 17th and 18th centuries, upper-class folks in Europe, particularly Great Britain, were preoccupied with the exploration of the world. Explorers sailed forth and returned, bringing, among other things, exotic plant specimens from around the globe. The study, cataloging, and propagation of these specimens fascinated generations of wealthy horticulturists, who built elaborate glass structures, known as *orangeries,* in which to grow and enjoy them.

In the Victorian era, the development of cast iron and advances in glass making brought down the cost of building sunrooms and conservatories. Now affordable for the middle classes, glass rooms remained popular until after World War I. After the war, however, the expense of heating and maintaining them began to weigh on the public consciousness, and their popularity dropped off significantly.

In the last decades of the 20th century, new materials and construction techniques once again made sunrooms and conservatories easier and less expensive to build and maintain. And once again, they became popular. Today, sunrooms, solariums, and conservatories of all sorts are popular remodeling projects and high on the list of amenities requested by homebuyers.

A rose by any other name may smell just as sweet, but the many names for porches and sunrooms are just plain confusing. Depending on the region of the world in which it's built, the very same structure could be referred to by half a dozen different terms.

To reduce potential confusion, here are definitions of common terms used in this book. Many other terms are common and quite correct, but these are the ones used here.

PORCH: roofed area with no more than three walls, at least one common to the house, and an open view of the outdoors. Also commonly known as a piazza, veranda, or gallery.

ENCLOSED PORCH: traditional porch with screens or simple windows added. Enclosed porches may project beyond the house but have at least one wall in common with the main structure.

PORTICO: covered entrance to a house. Includes at least one wall of the house and an entry door; open on at least one but usually two or three sides.

SUNROOM: room constructed of a collection of windows and a framed roof. A sunroom projects beyond the main structure and may have skylights.

SUN PORCHES: glass room that is part of the main footprint of the house; often has a full basement beneath.

SOLARIUM: lean-to structure made of glass that curves down from the ceiling to the floor.

CONSERVATORY: a structure with glass walls and a glass or transparent roof. Conservatories project beyond the main structure of the house.

How to use this book

The pages of *IdeaWise Porches & Sunrooms* are packed with images of porches and sunrooms. And while looking into other peoples homes and lives can be fun, we hope you'll do more than look at the photographs; we hope you'll study them carefully. We also hope you'll study the descriptions, facts, and details presented here—they're intended to help you plan a porch or sunroom project wisely.

Some of the porches and sunrooms in the book will suit your sense of style, while others may not appeal to you at all. If you're serious about remodeling or building a porch or sunroom, read it all—there's as much to learn in what you don't like as in what you do.

IdeasWise Porches & Sunrooms includes five chapters: Open Porches, Enclosed Porches, Sunrooms, Solariums, and Conservatories. In each chapter, you'll find several features, each of which contains a specific type of wisdom.

DesignWise

Robert Gerloff, AIA
Robert Gerloff residential Architects
Minneapolis, MN

• I'm the world's biggest fan of screen porches. You can only use them for three or four months in the summer, but during that time, they are absolutely perfect. Three-season porches may seem more logical—it makes sense to add windows to extend the time you can use the porch in the spring and fall—but my experience is that any glass traps in too much heat during the summer months, and I rarely see people enjoying three-season porches.

• Insulate the ceiling. Insulating a room that's open to the air may sound absurd, but most of the heat gain on a porch is from the sun heating up the roof and that heat then radiating into the porch itself. Insulating the roof will help keep the porch cooler.

• Most porches today are made with 2 x 6 decking

boards installed on the level rather than the traditional tongue-and-groove porch floors installed on a slope. You don't have to worry about water drainage, but be sure to install screens beneath the decking so mosquitoes and other bugs don't sneak into the porch through the spaces between boards.

• Keep sills low. Sills on a porch should ideally go down to the floor, or 18" off the floor at the absolute highest. The more open a porch, the more breeze it will collect and the cooler it will feel. The lower sills also make the porch feel more spacious.

• Plan your porch as close to your kitchen as possible. The easier it is to get another cool drink while sitting on the porch, the more the porch will be used. Family meals on the porch can also create cherished memories.

DollarWise

When you're home and the temperature is being controlled, sunroom accessories are protected from extremes. However, most of us set back our thermostats radically when we're away for extended periods, which can expose these accessories to major temperature shifts. Some accessories, such as candles and living plants, will melt or die in extreme heat. Protect your investment by pulling all shades and providing adequate ventilation or by removing these items from the sunroom while you're away.

IdeaWise

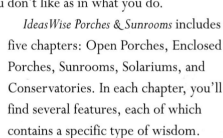

If you're adapting unique pieces into plant containers for your conservatory, remember that all planting containers must have drainage. If necessary, drill or punch several ¼" holes (spaced about 4" apart) in the bottom of the container, add a 2" layer of gravel, and fill the remainder of the container with potting soil. To drill holes in ceramic or glass, first use an awl to create a dimple, then drill the hole with a special glass-and-tile bit.

If you need to add a bottom to a container, try shaping hardware cloth to fit the opening. Secure the mesh with a wide bead of silicone caulk, and let it dry. Line the hardware cloth with sphagnum moss, and plant the container as usual.

CHAPTER 1

Open Porches

Modern porches are a mélange, an architectural stew of influences from all over the world—West Africa, India, the Mediterranean, Caribbean, and North America, to name a few. The result of centuries of mingled cultures and ideas, open porches balance at the border between indoors and out.

Porches give us front row seats for the parade of tiny changes in weather and landscape that mark the movement from one season to another, from one year to the next. From their vantage points, we can savor the sights, sounds, and smells of the world around us. A porch encourages us to simply be—with ourselves, with our loved ones, with the great outdoors.

Once you've embraced the idea of a porch, practical matters take center stage. Questions about location, orientation, materials, and style emerge; and the issue of budget begs to be considered. This chapter is filled with images and ideas that will guide and inform you as you plan, build, or decorate your porch.

"What I dream of is an art of balance." HENRI MATISSE

The design of the house and porch—identical windows on each side of the entry door, matching balusters on top and bottom railings, window boxes on each side of the broad staircase—establish a nice sense of balance for the whole. The bright container garden invites the eyes up and toward the porch.

Window boxes look lovely from the street or from inside the porch.

Trellis panels, painted to match the house, protect the underside of the porch without drawing attention to themselves.

White wicker looks cool and inviting.

Front Porches

First impressions of homes are as lasting as first impressions of people. An attractive front porch, the very essence of curb appeal, makes a good impression from near and far. From the street, a porch should look like a natural extension of the house rather than an afterthought. Trim details, roofing, and colors help a porch harmonize with the house; complementary furnishings and accessories create an immediate sense of welcome.

By its very nature, a front porch encompasses an entry door, often the main entrance to the house. To promote safety and security, the area should be well lighted and the landscaping trimmed to provide clear sight lines from the street.

Intricate details are the order of the day on this entry porch, too. The door, windows, and posts are emphasized with substantial millwork and pristine white enamel.

The beadboard ceiling is painted blue, a traditional color for porch ceilings. According to folklore, sky-blue ceilings discourage flies from hovering on porches. This may or not be true, but beautiful ceilings like this certainly encourage humans to linger.

A narrow porch shelters the entrance to this lovely home. The porch itself is rather plain, but elaborate trim details and a distinctive paint job give it the air of a storybook cottage.

Upstairs, the gables are defined by the narrow red trim and the keyhole-shaped windows and shutters. Downstairs, the door and windows are treated to the same generous trim details. Small red segments integrate the white porch posts into the overall design.

Repeated materials visually connect a porch to the house. Here, the stone face of the house is repeated on the porch. Masonry, such as stone, tile, or brick, is water resistant, which makes it an excellent material for porch floors. Two main factors to remember: masonry is heavy and requires strong structural support, and it's important to choose textured materials or to create a textured finish that will be slip resistant, even when wet. A masonry floor, like any other porch floor, must be sloped so that water runs away from the house.

Large masonry posts suit the style as well as the scale of the house. The gray color at the base coordinates with the gray trim above.

Framed by the curve of the soffit, the main entrance beckons visitors indoors.

The sleek curves of the porch roof are echoed in the metal balusters.

This contemporary porch and its furnishings are perfectly matched to the lines and spirit of the house. A simple black, white, and gray color scheme is carried from the paint and balustrade to the tables, chairs, and seating pieces. A brick floor warms the whole arrangement.

Small, simple posts complement the proportions of this porch.

Shrubs soften the strong rectilinear lines of this porch.

The placement of the entry door determines how a front porch will be used. Placing the door at the center divides the porch in half, which works nicely with large porches. Smaller porches, however, often benefit from another strategy: The stairs and entry are positioned on the near side of this small porch, leaving uninterrupted space for furnishings and accessories on the other.

The positions of the posts or columns play an important role in how the porch looks and what one sees from the porch. Here, the posts are positioned to frame the windows and door without interfering with the view from the windows. Building codes regulate the spacing of posts, but with careful planning, posts can be placed to enhance the view as well as the aesthetics of the porch.

A two-level porch complements the main entrance to this Swiss-style chalet. Standard square posts do the heavy lifting to support the second-floor porch, but more elaborate posts mark the entrance. The white-trimmed front door stands out nicely against the natural cedar clapboard siding.

The simple railing and wood floor help maintain the balance of the design.

Natural trim on the upstairs door helps it blend into the house rather than interrupting the flow of the design.

Swiss-style carvings dress the porch posts.

Matching balustrades visually tie together the two porches.

Pairs of columns top brick pillars to support the roof.

A pair of finials peeks over the land-scaping to help define the edges of the broad staircase.

The outstanding characteristic of this porch is its symmetry. Brick pillars topped by pairs of posts, broad stairs topped by a pair of urns, a pair of potted plants at the door—each of these paired elements plays a part in the well-balanced whole.

So, how do you know when symmetry is called for and when an asymmetrical arrangement would be more interesting? The house itself tells you. In this case, house is a model of symmetry: the doubled-door entrance is flanked by matching windows, a second porch tops the main one, and the color scheme is comprised of two strong colors. Adding symmetrical elements to this porch was a natural choice.

The glass panel in the door is divided by mullions similar to the ones in the window to the right.

This small porch contains an entry door at each end of the porch, a common situation. The homeowners focused attention on the main entrance by dressing it with substantial trim and contrasting paint, then they treated the second door to simple moldings and matching paint to help it recede into the background. The end result is a striking entrance and a gracious porch.

Vibrant flowering shrubs contribute spots of color to subtle color schemes.

The gentle curves of the arched trim soften the predominantly straight lines of the house and porch.

A brass toe kick provides a gleaming counterpoint to the black front door.

There are few pleasures as pure as a bright spring morning spent in a comfortable porch swing. Porch swings require plenty of support and should be installed only with substantial hardware and proper bracing.

*Design*Wise

Anthony & Liz Wilder
Anthony Wilder Design/Build, Inc.
Bethesda, Maryland

• When building a covered porch off of your house, always consider the potential loss of interior natural light: Rooms that were once very well lit, will undoubtedly lose much of their luminosity once the windows are beneath a covered porch. To avoid this loss of natural light, consider installing skylights over the windows.

• If you are using columns, be sure they are of proportionate size to the structure and the roof they are supporting.

• Make sure to up-light or down-light columns to accent the architectural elements.

• Consider installing one if not two ceiling fans to help circulate air.

• A wide, sweeping staircase and rail can add style to a traditional front porch.

• Choose synthetic materials for moldings, railings, columns, decking, and other architectural details. Synthetic materials are more durable than wood, and are low- to no-maintenance products.

Front porches are ideal locations for seasonal decorations. Here, the gable is draped with icicle lights and the balustrade festooned with garland, both of which enhance the home's gingerbread-trimmed façade.

The graceful details and pure white paint of this porch call for graceful, airy furnishings and accessories. The homeowners kept with the white theme for the basic pieces, then added colorful cushions. Fresh flowers and potted plants contribute additional spots of color.

Ceilings are key elements of good porch design.

An open ceiling softens the formality of this porch's massive columns. Often used in more rustic porches, open ceilings reveal the supporting rafters and the underside of the roof sheathing. Here, paint hides any imperfections in the lumber and blends the framing lumber into the monochromatic scheme of the porch.

Stained and sealed tongue-and-groove boards make a beautiful ceiling for the porch of this cedar-shake home.

The floor is the star of the show on this porch. A comfortable seat from which to enjoy the view is all that's necessary. Hardwood flooring may seem a surprising choice for a porch floor, but it's more practical than you might think. If you use a naturally moisture-resistant wood, such as mahogany, ipe (Brazilian hardwood), or teak and protect it with a high-quality sealer, you can have a stunning floor such as the one shown here. (If you want an exotic wood for your porch floor, choose a variety that has been sustainably grown and responsibly harvested.)

Good lighting contributes to the security of a porch as well as its appearance. Front porch lights should illuminate the steps as well as the entrance and provide a welcoming atmosphere for family and guests. Here, a hanging lantern adds ambience as well as light.

So nice they built it twice: a two-story porch provides the opportunity to enjoy cool breezes from upstairs bedrooms as well as from living areas of the house. Two-story porches present a gracious face to the world, but care must be taken to keep them from becoming imposing rather than welcoming.

The ceilings of large porches have to be adequately ventilated in order to keep moisture from building up inside the roof framing.

On the second floor, smaller columns top the stately first-floor columns, providing a nice sense of balance as well as a clear view above the railing.

Large porches call for large-scale fixtures such as this substantial lantern.

Bricks make outstanding porch floors, especially for ground-level porches where structural support isn't an issue. (Masonry floors are heavy and may require extra support on raised porches.)

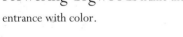

Flowering dogwoods frame the entrance with color.

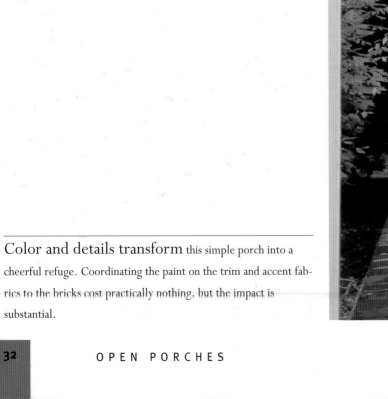

Color and details transform this simple porch into a cheerful refuge. Coordinating the paint on the trim and accent fabrics to the bricks cost practically nothing, but the impact is substantial.

The cedar shake siding has been sealed to retain its warm color. The shakes on the roof have been allowed to weather to gray.

Although the proportions are different, the bow window above the garage echoes the windows facing the porch.

Mullioned window lites in the garage door repeat a design motif from the bow windows.

Craftsman-style columns

and a simple balustrade frame the bow window facing this small-but-lovely porch. The details here are deliberately kept rather spare, in order to let the house and its setting shine. Repeated materials and shapes feature prominently in this design.

The boundaries of many porches are formed by railings. Another common style of porch features low walls, called *knee walls,* designed to work with the posts to support the weight of the roof.

Knee walls, often found on shingle-style houses and Craftsman bungalows, typically are covered with the same siding material as the house. They include drainage holes, known as *scuppers,* that let moisture drain away from the floor.

This house and its porch knee walls are covered with weathered cedar shingles. The posts and cap on the knee wall are painted turquoise to match the trim details on the house.

The knee wall continues to the back of the house, where it encloses a second porch.

Bright shutters draw attention to the windows, which are positioned above the top of the knee wall.

Back Porches

Back porches are special, elite in their own way. Most porches are relaxed, but back porches reach new heights in carefree living. Facing, as they often do, back yards, gardens, and pools, back porches include an extra dollop of comfort and ease. They're often used for dining and entertaining, as well as lounging.

Along with privacy, the relative seclusion of back porches brings unique challenges, such as safety and security. Windows facing a porch should be secured with sturdy locks and, if possible, connected to an alarm system. Landscaping should be planned with security in mind—don't plant large shrubs around doors or beneath windows unless they're extremely prickly or thorny. After all, there's no sense in providing hiding spots for potential burglars. Lighting should illuminate entrances and pathways.

Back porches play host to everything from casual dinners to elegant parties. When planning an entertaining space, ease of maintenance, durability, and adaptability are paramount.

This lovely space includes a round, stone-topped table and metal chairs, pieces that are incredibly durable and easy to maintain. With its white ceiling and simple brick floor, the neutral background of the porch works well with a wide variety of table settings and party themes.

A broad roof protects guests from sun and rain.

For parties, twinkle lights can be added to the trees.

Garlands, flowers, and other party decorations can be added to a trellis like this. Here, candle lanterns are suspended from the framing.

A fabric canopy transforms this porch into an intimate dining space, complete with flattering indirect lighting.

*Idea*Wise

Draped across a ceiling or hung across the end of a porch, gauzy fabric creates instant ambience. If you can use an iron, you can create fabric panels without sewing a stitch.

First, install large hooks in the ceiling or soffit; make sure the hooks are supported by studs or adequate anchors. Cut a 1" dowel to fit the opening.

Next, purchase enough fabric to fill the space. In order for the fabric to hang in graceful folds, you need about 1½ times the width of the opening. For example, if you're covering a 40" opening, one length of 60" wide fabric will work beautifully.

Use fusible seam tape to hem one end of the fabric and create a 2-inch rod pocket at the other. Slide the dowel into the rod pocket.

Suspend the dowel from the hooks, and your project is complete.

Comfortable chairs are a porch-side must, but don't forget the tables. They offer spots for serving drinks and snacks without taking up much space.

Weather-resistant fabrics resist fading and dry quickly, important qualities for porch furniture.

Coordinating a porch with its surroundings makes it appear to be a natural outcropping rather than a self-conscious addition. With its green trellises and neutral floor, this back porch blends effortlessly with the house and the lush garden beyond its perimeter.

The floor tile is similar in size to the paving stones used in the garden, but the color ties it to the house.

This elegant addition offers some-
thing for everyone: an open porch,
a screened porch, and a deck.

Natural materials help the porch
blend into the architecture of the classic
older home.

A comfortable seat, a cool morning, and a warm fire on the porch are a recipe for contentment.

Stone pillars topped with broad columns support the porch ceiling and screened porch above.

A wood ceiling glows overhead.

Flagstone makes a cool, low-maintenance floor for a ground-level porch like this.

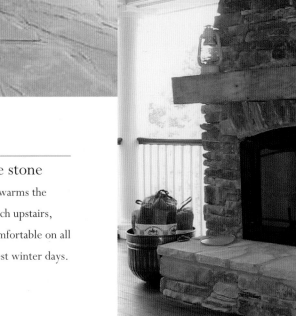

A massive stone fireplace warms the screened porch upstairs, making it comfortable on all but the coldest winter days.

With all due respect to Marshall McLuhan, sometimes the *material* is the message. Here, the unmilled tree trunks used as posts and bent twig furnishings deliver the rustic message started by the weathered siding and masonry floor.

(Note: Unmilled lumber must be very well dried before being used. This is an absolute requirement. Green timber shrinks as it dries, which would be a disaster in the making if used for posts like this.)

In the midst of all this rusticity, a sophisticated mantle provides contrast. When every piece in an area reflects the same style, period, or era, nothing stands out and the room becomes bland. Mixing styles, textures, and colors creates a welcome bit of drama.

Any porch with a corner has the potential to become an alcove like this.
By adding either a built-in banquette or a sectional sofa, you can turn a corner into a prize spot for entertaining, dining, or just relaxing in complete comfort.

Built-in banquettes can be designed with pullout drawers or lift-up lids so they offer storage as well as seating. Even weather-resistant cushions should be protected during long periods of bad weather, and built-in banquettes offer the perfect storage—sheltered and close at hand. (Note: cushions should be completely dry before being placed in storage.)

A dynamic arbor shelters this back porch, providing an interesting shape and texture as well as shade and some protection from wind and rain.

A sun canopy shades this broad, terrace-like back porch. The clear ceiling panels provide shelter without sacrificing the light or the view.

A roof extension further protects the seating area from sun and rain.

A soaring cathedral ceiling encloses this dramatic back porch. A fireplace positioned at one end chases away morning and evening chills and warms the space visually as well.

Built-in wood storage keeps the area neat.

A natural-fiber rug provides a rich foundation for the white and black color scheme of the furnishings and accessories.

The stone of the fireplace surround is repeated as window trim.

Candles add warmth to the cozy atmosphere.

The floor tile complements—but does not match—the fireplace and window trim.

This porch includes both a gas fireplace and an "electronic hearth," as some people refer to a television. Although most porches are places to escape the intrusion of sounds not found in nature, this is an exceptionally fine place to curl up and watch a favorite old movie or to indulge in a glass of wine along with the evening news.

Wrap-around Porches

Wrap-around porches typically surround at least two sides of the house and often serve more than one entry to the house. This type of porch multiplies your options: If the sun is too bright or the wind too strong on one side, there may be respite on another. One area may be reserved for activities such as dining or entertaining, while another serves as space for rest and relaxation.

Typical urban and suburban houses are close to the lot lines. Pay careful attention to setback restrictions when planning a wrap-around porch or other porch attached to the side of a house.

Fanciful trim details draw attention to the sweeping curve of the wrap-around porch on this Queen Anne-style Victorian home. Panels on the front door have been painted to match the fascia, an imaginative and attractive detail. Concrete urns are filled with color-coordinated blooming plants.

The elaborate trim work of this wrap-around porch give this simple house a charming outlook. The white paint on the gingerbread plays well with the subtle-but-cheery taupe, white, and cranberry color scheme of the exterior.

Shrubs and lush perennials hide the porch's underpinnings.

Both the primary and secondary entries open onto the front porch.

Pairs of corbels give presence to the shallow soffit.

Wide, open steps welcome visitors.

This porch doesn't just wrap around, it embraces the house. The gentle curve of the soffit and railing are emphasized by the looping garland and manicured hedge.

The house and porch share a subtle color scheme that allows the furnishings and accessories to take center stage.

A deep, wide porch is best suited by large plants and planters, such as this potted palm.

Scale is an important consideration when designing or adding a porch, especially one that surrounds the house. Here, the sheer mass of the porch calls for substantial details. The architects answered the call by providing broad moldings, hefty columns, and wide, open stairs.

From the structure—the posts, balusters, and trim—to the color scheme, every element of a porch should complement the house itself. Carefully selected furnishings and accessories, including peacock wicker chairs and colorful carousel horses, create a fanciful atmosphere for a porch that wraps around this lovingly maintained Victorian house.

Highlighting the window trim with an accent color brings a special sparkle to each pane.

The cream and green color scheme is carried from the house to the porch and even its furnishings.

Repeating materials from the house in the landscape structures blends the two, but that's not always possible when working with an older home. These retaining walls are made of a stone not found on the house, but the wall's brick-colored cap and matching steps are enough to tie the walls into the design scheme.

The porch roof includes a gable that echoes the relative scale and pitch of the gable on the main house.

Evergreens are shaped in inverse proportion to the shape and scale of the porch posts and trim.

Grand double staircases lead to the porch, a detail that draws focus to the main entrance of the house.

Porch floors are built to slope gently away from the house—typically a slope of about one-quarter inch per horizontal foot—and have weather-resistant floor coverings.

Unpainted, untreated wood floors need to be given a coat of preservative before they're installed and every two or three years after that. Even treated wood should be sealed every couple of years.

A unique Z-shaped porch wraps this Victorian home in color and comfort.
The simple swing hanging beside the front door offers an ideal spot for relaxing on a lazy afternoon.

Porch swings require adequate structural support and sturdy hanging hardware. The best time to decide on a porch swing is during the construction process, when it's easy to add additional joists or blocking. It's possible, but not easy, to add blocking to an existing porch.

When a porch wraps to the side of a house, it's often quite close to a neighboring home, which makes privacy an issue. There are many ways to create privacy, including lattice panels and other types of screening.

Simple log posts support the broad roof of the wrap-around porch on this log home. The stone foundation of the porch is in perfect keeping with the rustic materials and style of this home.

A lattice panel at one end screens the seating area from view.

A tree shades two sides of the porch while the third side gets more sun.

Lattice aprons dress the space between the foundation's piers and keep critters from taking up residence beneath the porch.

The simple white posts and balusters of this wrap-around porch make lovely counterpoints to the house's unique marine-blue siding.

Railing requirements—including the height of the railing and the spacing of balusters—are determined by local building codes. Typically, railings are required if the porch floor is 30" or more above ground; stair railings are generally required for more than two steps. Complying with all local building regulations protects the safety of your family as well as the security of the investment you're making in the porch.

Hanging flower baskets, wind chimes, and bird feeders are popular porch accessories.

Epoxy-modified acrylic latex paint on the floor stands up to heavy traffic and cleans up with soap and water.

Everything from the picket fence to the plantings focuses all eyes on the entrance to this porch.

Trim details are repeated from one level to the next.

Downspouts hide in plain sight, running down the posts from the second-story gutters to splashguards on the ground below.

A grand staircase leads from one porch to the other, encouraging guests to use both.

Lattice panels keep debris and animals out from under the porch floor.

This two-story wrap-around porch offers family and guests an extra opportunity to relish the luxurious landscaping surrounding the house. Because the first floor porch is above ground level, there is a railing there as well as on the second story.

CHAPTER 2

Enclosed Porches

Flies, mosquitoes, gnats, and no-see-ums of all sorts have been bugging humans since time began. Porches are especially common in warm, humid climates, the very regions where bugs are at their worst. Enclosed porches give us the benefits of being outdoors without the irritations.

At the time of the Civil War, soldiers began weaving horsehair into screen for sieves and strainers. After the war, some enterprising soul realized this screen could be used to "strain" the air, and screen-filled frames soon surrounded porches across the land. Although horsehair soon gave way first to wire and later to fiberglass mesh, not much else about screened porches has changed in the intervening years.

It's a small step from screened to glass-enclosed porches, often referred to as "three-season porches" because they provide protection from wind and rain but not cold. Some trend watchers say that interest in three-season porches has dwindled in recent years, citing the small difference in costs between three- and four-season porches. Others contend that interest remains strong.

What experts say doesn't matter; what does matter is choosing the type of porch that suits your home and lifestyle. In this chapter, you'll encounter many ideas and examples that will help you make those choices.

Converting a deck into a screened porch is a relatively reasonable project in terms of both time and expense. The structural support for a deck typically is adequate for a screened porch. The chief concerns are framing the roof and walls.

Gutters and downspouts direct rainwater away from the porch and house.

Screening the underside of a raised porch floor keeps bugs out but still lets water drain away.

Most building codes require railings or kneewalls on porches more than 30" off the ground.

Screen panels, often black or charcoal to reduce glare, tend to darken a space. These windows bring additional light to the porch as well as to the room beyond the porch.

Screen comes in 60" widths, but most experts recommend using panels of 42" or less. Smaller panels are easier and less expensive to repair than large ones.

Enclosed porches blend the best of indoor and outdoor life.

Screened Porches

Screen itself is the basis of a screened porch. These days, most screen is made of aluminum or fiberglass. Each type has advantages and disadvantages: Fiberglass is lightweight, easy to work with, and keeps its color over time. Its chief disadvantage is that it permanently changes shape if stressed, leading to bulges and stretched places. Aluminum is more durable and less likely to be stretched out of shape, but it discolors with age.

Screen comes in black or charcoal as well as lighter gray. Darker screen reduces glare, but lighter screen interferes less with the view and lets in more light. You can also get copper and bronze screen, which is extremely durable. The problem is these materials costs up to 10 times as much as aluminum and fiberglass. You could replace standard screens many times before spending an amount equal to the cost of more exotic screening materials.

A ceiling fan is a welcome addition to a porch with an open ceiling.

These folding tables are easy to store when bad weather sets in.

Screen porches are sheltered spaces, but furnishings and accessories still need to be weather-resistant, such as these wicker chairs.

Railings and walls aren't required on ground-level porches, but unsupported screens are easily damaged. Here, screen panels are raised slightly above the floor and supported by a rail at kneewall height.

Rather than attaching the screen to the framing members, many designers suggest building individual screen panels that fit into the framing. If a panel is damaged, it can be easily removed and repaired.

Many screened porches are built with solid panels about 36" high, which protect the screen without significantly diminishing the view or reducing access to cool breezes. The panels on this porch also include narrow reinforcements to support the screen. The better supported a screen is, the fewer repairs will be necessary. If a panel is damaged, it can be easily removed and repaired.

A beadboard ceiling with a coat of traditional blue paint creates a calm, cool atmosphere.

Lamps and other electrical fixtures on screened porches should be plugged into GFCI-protected receptacles.

Potted plants brighten a porch but require frequent watering in order to thrive in an environment that includes wind but limited access to moisture.

The durable, painted concrete floor is covered by a weather-resistant sisal rug, an excellent choice for screened porches.

Even with sturdy locks, screened porches offer little security. Install deadbolt locks on the doors leading to the house, and keep them locked at night and when you're away.

This screened porch is set up to withstand almost any weather. The furnishings were selected with an eye to weather resistance—a wooden screen shelters the lamp, and the concrete pad is sloped to shed water.

Adding a concrete pad for a screened porch is a labor-intensive but manageable do-it-yourself project. If you're lucky enough to have an existing patio, building a screened porch over it can be quite inexpensive since the slab and footings already exist. If you're not absolutely sure your slab or patio is adequately supported, check with a qualified contractor, building inspector, or architect before building on it.

The hipped roof of this broad porch shelters the room from the glaring sun.

When planning a porch, consider its orientation and how it will affect your home's interior. In sunny, warm climates, a south- or west-facing porch shades the interior and reduces the cost of cooling. In less sunny regions or on the north or east side of a house, a porch can cut off much-needed light and warmth.

The framework of this second-story screened porch creates an open porch below, a happy combination that offers the best of both porch worlds.

Dark screen reduces glare, but they can darken the interior too much. To combat that problem, this screened porch includes screens all the way up to the peak of the gable and a skylight on each side of the roof.

Lattice panels enclose the bottom of the porch. Even with panels like this, the underside of the floor needs to be screened or otherwise protected from invading insects.

Set adjacent to both the kitchen and the grilling area on the deck, this screened porch provides ideal space for dining and entertaining.

A standard porch light illuminates the porch without the expense of additional wiring.

With its casual appearance and weather resistance, traditional patio furniture is perfect for a screened porch.

*Design*Wise

Robert Gerloff, AIA
Robert Gerloff residential Architects
Minneapolis, MN

• I'm the world's biggest fan of screen porches. In northern climates you can only use them for three or four months in the summer, but during that time, they are absolutely perfect. Three-season porches may seem more logical—it makes sense to add windows to extend the time you can use the porch in the spring and fall—but my experience is that any glass traps in too much heat during the summer months, and I rarely see people enjoying three-season porches.

• Insulate the ceiling. Insulating a room that's open to the air may sound absurd, but most of the heat gain on a porch is from the sun heating up the roof and that heat then radiating into the porch itself. Insulating the roof will help keep the porch cooler.

• Most porches today are made with 2 x 6 decking boards installed on the level rather than the traditional tongue-and-groove porch floors installed on a slope. You don't have to worry about water drainage, but be sure to install screens beneath the decking so mosquitoes and other bugs don't sneak into the porch through the spaces between boards.

• Keep sills low. Sills on a porch should ideally go down to the floor, or 18" off the floor at the absolute highest. The more open a porch, the more breeze it will collect and the cooler it will feel. The lower sills also make the porch feel more spacious.

• Plan your porch as close to your kitchen as possible. The easier it is to get another cool drink while sitting on the porch, the more the porch will be used. Family meals on the porch can also create cherished memories.

There's no rule that screen panels have to be boring. Here, a geometric arrangement of square and rectangular panels creates a porch with striking good looks.

Placing a large square panel in the center of each wall of the porch preserved much of the view from inside the porch.

With its special railing, this porch shows its style from inside and out.

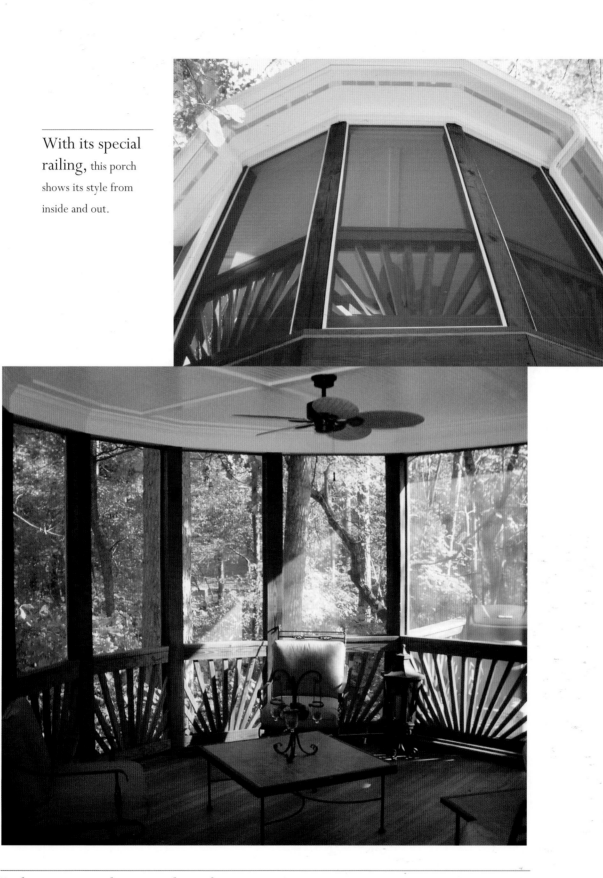

Railings, essential on raised porches, can be used to add interest to otherwise simple designs.

This octagonal porch is made up of simple rectangles, which might have been bland without the sunburst railing.

Three-season Porches

Three-season porches are enclosed with partial walls, single-glazed windows, and a door. Typically, the walls, windows, and doors aren't insulated, and the enclosure isn't served by the house's heating or air conditioning systems. With recent improvements in window and door technology, three-season porches aren't much less expensive to build than sunrooms. Still, many people prefer three-season rooms because they're experienced as true porches rather than simply living areas with lots of windows.

The roof sheds water easily; gutters direct rainwater away from the house and foundation.

Screens keep out the bugs when the windows are opened during temperate weather.

Lattice panels provide air circulation beneath the porch.

Lean-to porches are popular because they're relatively inexpensive to build and easy to maintain. Lean-to designs can be adapted to fit even small spaces. This modest porch adds a surprising amount of sunny space to the back of the house.

This porch is furnished for casual meals and leisurely evenings filled with lamplight and good conversation. That's the magic of porches: they remove distances between people and create distance from distractions.

Truly a three-season affair, the glass enclosure buffers the wind and rain, but the air on the porch is still warm or cool, according to the season. Thanks to the porch, the home's interior is cooler in summer and warmer in winter than it would otherwise be.

Three-season porches need to be oriented to suit not only the house, but also the climate. In cold-weather regions, a three-season porch with a southern or western exposure can be comfortable in all but the coldest weather. In warm-weather regions, an eastern exposure provides cheery sunny mornings and avoids late-day blasts of sun.

The table is laid for lunch in this lovely porch. With a breeze wafting through that open door, this is the finest spot in the house for midday meal.

Houseplants thrive
in the sunny comfort
of the porch's windows.
Here, abundant greenery ac-
cents a vintage console.

Vintage hardware doesn't offer much security. Make sure the entry doors beyond the porch have sturdy deadbolts.

Removable window sashes are easy to clean and maintain. If a pane is broken or damaged, it simply can be removed and taken to the hardware store for repairs.

Painted wood makes an easy-care, no-hassle porch floor. Epoxy-reinforced porch floor paint stands up to years of use between coats.

Skylights add wonderful, diffused light to a porch but need to be placed carefully. In warm climates, avoid south-or west-facing skylights, or choose units that can be shaded when necessary.

*Idea*Wise

You can create a lovely candle chandelier for a screen or three-season porch used for dining. Start with a moss-lined hanging basket filled with trailing vines and flowers. Add brass candle spikes around the perimeter of the basket.

Suspend the flowering chandelier 34 to 36" above the dining table. Especially when wet, the basket will be heavy: anchor the hanging hardware into a ceiling joist or use heavy-duty anchors.

Skylights shed light on the rather dark interior of this large screened porch.

In a typical enclosed porch, the house's siding is visible on at least one wall. Here, white siding merges with the white walls and ceiling.

The skylights create a cheerful, sunny space, but that can be a mixed blessing. During cool weather, solar gain is an advantage, but in hot weather, it can make a porch uncomfortably warm. By circulating warm air in the winter and generating a breeze in the summer, a ceiling fan makes a porch more comfortable no matter what the weather.

Sunrooms

The words sunroom and sun porch conjure up a variety of images and interpretations. For our purposes, a sunroom is constructed of a collection of windows and a framed roof that projects beyond the main structure and may have skylights or transparent panels in the roof; a sun porch is a glassed-in room that's part of the main footprint of the house.

Large areas of glass open sunrooms and sun porches to the beauty of the sky and sun and surrounding landscape. Like any porches, they are bridges between indoors and out, but unlike open porches, their climates are controlled by heating and air conditioning systems.

When planning a sunroom or sun porch, two issues are critical: integration and orientation. A sunroom should blend into the existing architecture so it looks and acts like an original part of the house; it should be positioned, or oriented, to take advantage of available sunlight and views.

This chapter presents dozens of examples of sunrooms and sun porches to inform and inspire you.

Sunrooms

Sunrooms, sometimes called four-season porches, are distinguished from other sunny rooms by their access to light and air. Because their walls project beyond the main structure of the house, sunrooms provide panoramic views of the surrounding landscape.

This raised sunroom rests between two decks, offering terrific possibilities for family gatherings and large parties.

An operable skylight provides additional light and ventilation.

Well-insulated walls and ceilings control both comfort and energy costs.

The interior design, featuring hardwood floors and traditional furnishings, flows well with adjoining rooms.

Sliding windows provide excellent ventilation. Energy-efficient thermal glass reduces heating and cooling costs.

Electric baseboard heat keeps the sunroom comfortable in cold weather.

Sunrooms bring the outside in.

The glass walls and ceiling of this expansive sunroom give you the feeling you're living in the yard—minus the bugs and uncomfortable weather, of course.

Operable skylights and a ceiling fan improve the room's ventilation.

Special glazing techniques protect sunrooms and their furnishings from sun damage.

A micro-lam beam supports the broad expanse of the roof.

Two sets of French doors provide easy access and fresh breezes to the patio.

Tile floors are naturally cool in the summer and, with the addition of radiant heat, warm in the winter.

The shape, size, and style of a sunroom should complement the house rather than dominate it.

From the pitch of the roof to the siding and deck materials to the shape and size, this sunroom is perfectly tailored to the home. Although substantial in size, it appears to be a natural extension to the house rather than an abrupt addition.

Dark trim and stone walls flow from the house to the sunroom, integrating it into the whole.

The gables, overhangs, roofing materials, siding, and windows of this sunroom make it a logical extension of the main house. Even the bedding plants play a part in blending the two.

This sunroom extends the house toward the mountains. Carrying materials, such as this hardwood flooring, from the main house to the sunroom integrates the two with ease.

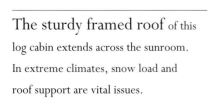Insulated glass and modern construction methods make a sunroom comfortable in any weather.

The sturdy framed roof of this log cabin extends across the sunroom. In extreme climates, snow load and roof support are vital issues.

This sunroom offers a lovely spot from which to observe wildlife or simply take in the ever-changing view of the mountains.

In warm climates, keeping a sunroom cool is the challenge. Insulated glass, special glazing techniques, and good ventilation are the keys to year-round comfort. Proper orientation is also critical: avoid southern or western exposures unless the sunroom will be shaded at least part of the day. Here, mature trees provide dappled shade for the sunroom.

*Idea*Wise

Plants and sunrooms are a natural pairing, and hanging plants, such as ferns and ivy, are particularly appealing. Rather than installing dozens of hooks for plants, hang a rod or dowel along a beam and suspend the baskets along it. Use chain or hook accessories to vary the heights of the baskets.

In extreme climates of all sorts, a framed roof with skylights may be the wisest option. A roof like the one here is built to withstand even the heaviest snow loads and remain cool beneath the hottest sun.

Orientation, or the placement of the sunroom, is vital to climate control. Typically, the goal is to maximize the amount of sunlight it receives, but that isn't always possible or even desirable, depending on the characteristics of the house, lot, and climate.

• North-facing sunrooms, which receive little direct sunlight, don't require sun control measures but can be expensive to heat. Excellent insulation is important.

• South-facing sunrooms receive sunlight most of the day and so can get very hot in summer. They need operable windows and roof vents to provide ventilation and air circulation. Window treatments and tinted glass help to protect the room and its furnishings.

• East-facing sunrooms receive a good deal of morning sun but little in the afternoon. Unless you're a consistently early riser, this is not the best orientation for a sunroom adjoining a bedroom, but it's lovely for a breakfast or sitting room.

• West-facing sunrooms receive direct sun in the afternoon and early evening and, like south-facing rooms, can get very hot. But with adequate insulation, ventilation and air circulation, west-facing sunrooms can be exceptionally pleasant.

Plants and people thrive in the abundant sunshine available in this sunroom.

Sunrooms offer dining rooms with a view.

A casement window opens the sunroom to prevailing breezes.

A deadbolt lock provides a measure of security for this door. In out-of-the-way locations, a security system can be a good addition.

A glass corner cabinet holds crystal without spoiling the view.

The kitchen floor extends into the sunroom, with a two-step transition. The dark strip emphasizes the steps and makes them easier to navigate.

Every meal is special when accompanied by a spectacular view like this. An auxiliary dining area has been established on the deck, but the sunroom hosts meals in any weather, year-round.

This airy, sun-filled sunroom is open to the kitchen and provides space for both casual and formal dining.

The dining furniture suits the room perfectly. The glass tabletop has little visual weight and the complementary wood tones and light upholstery on the chairs keep them from interfering with the view.

Positioned at a pass-through to the kitchen, the breakfast bar is a great spot for snacks or quick meals.

*Dollar*Wise

When you're home and the temperature is being controlled, sunroom accessories are protected from extremes. However, most of us set back our thermostats radically when we're away for extended periods, which can expose these accessories to major temperature shifts. Some accessories, such as candles and living plants, will melt or die in extreme heat. Protect your investment by pulling all shades and providing adequate ventilation or by removing these items from the sunroom while you're away.

This casual dining space offers the best of both worlds. It's open to the spectacular garden view but sheltered from direct sun by translucent ceiling panels. The sunroom windows are aligned with the windows of the house to create views from inside as well as out.

With their casual styles and sunny aspects, sunrooms make ideal enclosures for pools, hot tubs, and spas.

A gallery of windows embraces a lap pool, providing a comfortable environment for workouts in any weather.

Exposed framing and transparent panels enclose a pool and spa area, protecting it from the weather without eliminating the light and views.

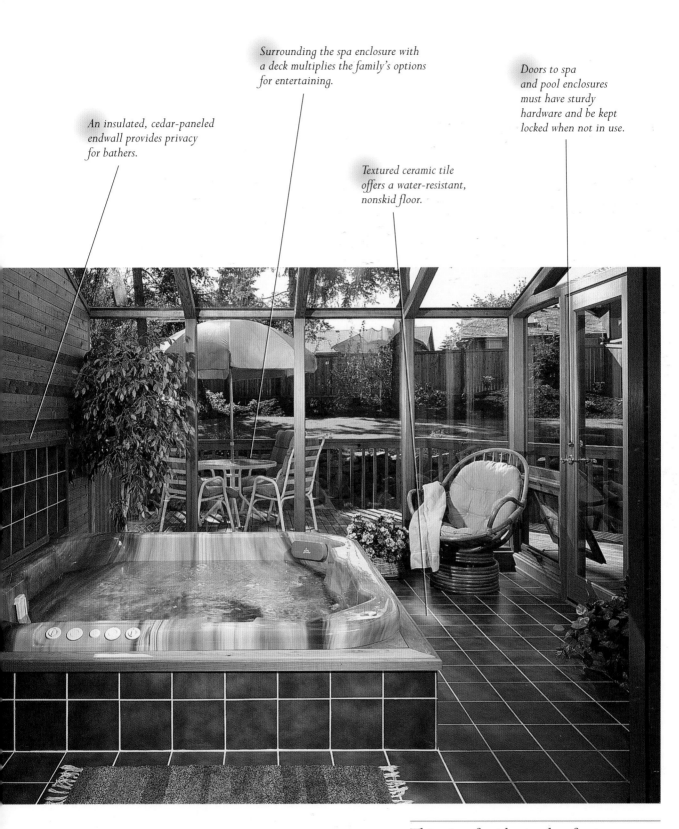

An insulated, cedar-paneled endwall provides privacy for bathers.

Surrounding the spa enclosure with a deck multiplies the family's options for entertaining.

Textured ceramic tile offers a water-resistant, nonskid floor.

Doors to spa and pool enclosures must have sturdy hardware and be kept locked when not in use.

This nine-foot by twelve-foot sunroom
encloses a luxurious spa tub and sitting area.

Sun Porches

A sun porch is a glassed-in room that's part of the main footprint and open to the rest of the house. Common in older homes, sun porches are making a comeback similar to that of open porches as home builders and remodelers respond to buyers' growing preference for a connection between a house and the world surrounding it.

The flat roof doubles as a floor for the second-story deck.

Pairs of French doors open onto a deck.

Surrounded by charming decks, this sun porch opens the house to the sights, sounds, and smells of the lovely back yard.

Both plants and people luxuriate in this sun-drenched room on the side of the house. With its high, glass ceiling and sliding glass doors, the sun porch offers a view of the yard and a delightful environment for the homeowners and their friends.

The cool stone floors and broad French doors of this sun porch
create an elegant but intimate atmosphere where plants can thrive and guests can relax
in comfort.

If you're lucky enough to have a space like this in your home, make the most of it.
Add lush green plants and garden statuary. Play up the porch aspect by using wrought
iron, rattan, or other furniture traditionally used outdoors. Keep window treatments
simple. Better yet, leave the windows bare if privacy isn't an issue.

The cool terra-cotta floor of this sun porch sets the tone for a Southwestern-style room. Native American patterns, rustic tables, and colorful accessories complete the picture.

*Design*Wise

Colin and Debi Hawkes
Buena Vista Sunrooms
Ventura, CA

• Learn about your glass options. Many factors affect the energy efficiency of the glass: the type and thickness of the glass, the amount of space between the panes, and the addition of argon gas between the panes. Low-emissivity glass has a microscopically thin metallic coating on the inside face of the outer pane which stops radiant heat flow and can greatly reduce the amount of potentially damaging ultraviolet light that enters the room. Windows with a low-E rating will also have a low U-value (which indicates its resistance to heat flow. The lower the U-value, the less heat flows through the glass. Laminated glass blocks most of the UV light, which is the component that fades fabrics and furniture.

• Add a ridge vent. Ridge vents on the roof are very effective ways to reduce the heat build-up. Hot air rises, so combined with windows, ridge vents provide a passive cooling system that works well.

• Think about choosing a solid or partially solid, insulated roof. A glass roof is attractive, but how are you going to clean it? Also, make sure the pitch of the roof is steep enough that leaves and dirt will slide off easily.

• Consider a "folding glass wall," a series of attached 3' doors, rather than sliding glass doors. These folding glass walls can be installed to fold like an accordion to one side or the other, or can be split down the middle, which opens up the entire space.

The designers truly made the most of a relatively small space in this spectacular two-story sun porch. The second floor is accessible via the space-saving spiral staircase, and a luxurious container garden is tucked into its curves. Matching the floor tile to the wall and trim color further expands the room. The compact wicker furniture provides comfortable seating without taking up too much space.

Uncontrolled sun can discolor or damage furniture, fabrics and artwork. Blinds, which give you the option for full light, filtered light or blocked light, are a traditional solution to the problem. These window treatments give you plenty of options. You can pull the blinds up completely for a clear view, lower the blinds but open the louvers to filter the sun, or lower the blinds and close the louvers to block the sun entirely.

Recessed lights spotlight the artwork.

This long, narrow sun porch functions as a breakfast room for the homeowners. What a way to start the day: surrounded by sunshine and great art.

Be careful about the type of art you display in a sun porch or any other room open to abundant natural light. Direct sun may fade or damage some works. Don't hang them in direct sun, and use light-filtering window treatments when necessary. If you're not sure about the durability of a favorite piece, check with an art dealer or gallery for specific instructions.

Roller shades on the windows block the sun when necessary or retract almost completely.

CHAPTER 4

Solariums

The word *solarium* has its roots in the Latin word for sun, *sol.* Generally speaking, any sunny, glassed-in room or porch can be called a solarium, but in this chapter, we're going to explore one particular style—lean-to structures that curve down from ceiling to floor.

Historically, solariums were included in hospitals and convalescent centers so that patients could bask in the sun, which was known to speed recuperation. At one time, the high cost of building and maintaining a solarium kept them limited to public buildings and the homes of the very rich, but modern materials and components have made it possible to include these sunny spaces in homes across the economic spectrum.

Solariums provide climate-controlled, year-round living space often used as a breakfast room, sitting room, or home office. Solariums also frequently enclose spas and pools. Throughout this chapter, you'll see many imaginative, inventive ways solariums can be included in or added to a home.

Although exterior doors are optional, this solarium has a door that opens to the surrounding patio and garden. Give careful thought to where your solarium will be located, how it will be used, and what the traffic patterns are likely to be as you consider whether or not to include doors.

Grade-level solariums are built on slab or perimeter foundations with footings that extend below the frost line, as defined by local building codes. The foundation is poured and allowed to cure, and then the solarium is assembled.

The brick kneewall complements the brick patio.

The patio slopes down and away from the solarium to direct water away from the foundation.

A sliding door opens onto the patio and garden.

With plenty of track lighting and remote-controlled shades, light can be adjusted to suit the needs of the moment in this home office/studio. When planning a solarium that will be used as an office, consider the environmental requirements of the electronic components that will be housed there, as well as the comfort of the users.

A bench extending from the kneewall provides a lovely seat from which to observe the landscape.

This solarium was designed as a hobby greenhouse, a wonderful addition for any devoted gardener. The slatted wooden benches hold flats of seedlings in the spring and plants that need extra TLC any time of year. Space beneath the benches accommodates gardening tools and supplies.

Plan for comfort in every season.

It doesn't matter whether you're trying to deflect extreme heat or cold, good materials and construction methods are your best ally. To reduce energy consumption and ensure comfort, select a solarium designed for your climate. Glass options include mirrored, tinted, and insulated glass, as well as insulated glass filled with an inert gas, such as argon.

This solarium, found in Taos, New Mexico, was carefully designed to suit its location. To combat heat gain, the designers mounted it on a 30" high base wall and included automatic roof vents controlled by a thermostat. The glass, including the curves, is tempered safety glass.

This solarium includes, as do many grade-level versions, a kneewall. Kneewalls raise the joint between the solarium unit and the foundation, which protects it from melting snow and rain. They also provide space to conceal wiring and ductwork, and they incorporate matching or complementary siding to help blend the solarium into the existing structure.

In a climate such as this, snow load is a concern: both the materials and the construction must be designed to withstand substantial weight.

This solarium, tucked into a corner of the house,
is a warm, sunny retreat in any weather. By orienting the solarium
properly, sheltering one side with the house, and super-insulating the
floor, the designers were able to create an energy-efficient, year-
round environment.

Bathe in sunshine.

Solariums that enclose bathing
spaces have special considerations,
such as privacy and ventilation. Most spas or bathrooms need blinds or shades. In this bathroom, the
blinds can be drawn in a privacy zone without
completely shutting out the view.

Here, the blinds
slide down from
the ceiling to ensure
complete privacy. Re-
mote control blinds are
convenient in solariums,
especially because they
eliminate the unattractive
mess of cords and hooks.

This spa area has sliding windows that can be opened for fresh air, but mechanical ventilation is still essential. The ventilation system for any bathing space must be rated to handle the square footage of the room. Consult an HVAC (heating, ventilation, and air conditioning) specialist familiar with the special requirements of both solariums and spas or bathrooms.

The bronze finish on this solarium complements the trim color of the house as well as the leafy setting.

This highly unusual solarium suits the house beautifully. The graceful arches echo the scrolls of the light fixtures and the balcony railings. The trellis-like shakes filter light without eliminating it and protect the solarium from solar gain.

When it comes to a successful solarium design, it's all about integration. The solarium should be added to the house as seamlessly as possible, and that means using matching or complementary siding on knee-walls, selecting colors that fit the exterior color scheme of the house, and landscaping in such a way so as to blend the solarium into the picture.

Window-box planters surround the solarium as well as the other first-floor windows of this white stucco home.

The white trim and tinted windows help this solarium blend into the structure of the house. Foundation plantings soften the edges of the structure, and graceful urns emphasize the entrance.

The weight of a raised **solarium** is supported by posts and footings that reach well below the frost line, as defined by local building codes. The supporting structure is much like that of a deck, but it must be designed especially to support the weight of the solarium.

To keep energy costs in check, the floor of a raised solarium must be well insulated. This is a situation wherein radiant floor heat might be especially appropriate.

*Idea*Wise

No matter how much space we have, it seems like we can never have too much storage. If your solariun has knee-walls, here's an easy, attractive way to add storage. Frame out a bench, about 18" high, 18" deep, and at least 4' long, and anchor it to the kneewall. Top the bench with a hinged lid and add an upholstered cushion.

The storage space inside is sure to be welcome, as is the front-row seat for the view from the solarium.

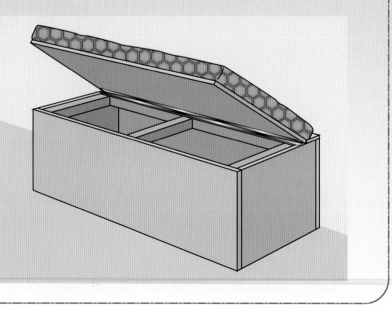

This spacious solarium houses a seating area as well as a casual dining space. In a solarium with a ceramic tile floor, radiant heat is an option worth considering. Radiant heat systems keep ceramic tile floors toasty, even in the coldest weather.

This ceiling fan also includes light fixtures to illuminate the dining area. A dimmer allows users to adjust the light level to the occasion.

Dark molding, stained to complement the furnishings, frames the solid walls of the solarium.

Operable windows and two ceiling fans provide fresh air and ventilation for the space.

*Design*Wise

Al Meffan
Patio Enclosures, Inc.
Macedonia, Ohio

• Plan, plan, plan. Consider the region's climate, the room's orientation to sunlight, the presence of shade, and the expected use of the space when deciding whether a solarium is the best option for your home. There is no "bad" orientation for a solarium, but northern exposures present different challenges than southern exposures. Any site can be ideal with the proper selection of ventilation options and mechanical systems.

• Choose high-quality materials. Most solariums intended as living space (as opposed to horticultural greenhouses) are constructed with double-pane insulating glass in the walls as well as the roof. They include thermal breaks in most if not all of the framing members and generally are built on insulated foundations. Because of the large expanse of glass, tempered panes are best.

• Provide good ventilation. Proper HVAC equipment makes a room more enjoyable and less expensive to maintain. Adding a

door to separate the solarium from the rest of the house maximizes energy efficiency.

• Choose blinds and shades that complement the decorating. Blinds and shades are also used to filter light, control heat gain, and enhance privacy and security. The most often popular shades are fabric or PVC blinds, but pleated shades are also an option.

• Install attractive floor coverings. Solarium floors pose no specific limitations, with the most appropriate choice being dictated by intended use and personal taste. Gone are the days of indoor/outdoor grass cloth. Today's choices include anything from carpet and ceramic tile to laminate and hardwood flooring.

• Create a plan for electrical fixtures. Duplex receptacles, phone jacks, feeds for cable TV and stereo speakers, as well as outdoor spotlights and interior ceiling fans may be desirable. Once again, a solarium's electrical needs will vary based on individual requirements.

Opening onto an expansive bedroom, this solarium provides comfortable space for relaxing with a cup of coffee in the morning or star gazing at night.

A solarium opening to a bedroom usually requires substantial blinds or shades for both privacy and sun control. In a room such as this, the entire space could be closed off with drawable draperies or other window treatments.

A partial wall anchors the bed and provides a place to spotlight a treasured piece of artwork.

A ceiling fan supplies a cool breeze over the bed.

Although the solarium is fully climate controlled, a freestanding fireplace is a cozy addition.

Music and nature are a perfect combination, but musical instruments and extreme conditions are not. If you plan to use your solarium as a music room, consult experts regarding the temperature, humidity, and sun exposure precautions necessary to protect your instruments.

Here, a combination of effective ventilation, shade, and an efficient HVAC system create a hospitable environment for the musician, the piano, and an audience. The solarium floor is reinforced to support the large piano.

CHAPTER 5

Conservatories

olonel Mustard. With a candlestick. In the Conservatory.

The board game "Clue" may be the closest many of us have ever been to a conservatory, possibly because we have the impression that they are vaguely British, very upper-crust, and probably beyond our means. While that may once have been true, conservatories are found all around the globe today.

Originally developed to protect or "conserve" plant specimens brought back from exotic destinations during the reign of King George III, the first conservatories were expensive wrought-iron-and-glass creations that only the upper classes could afford to build or maintain. Today, new materials such as aluminum, metal-reinforced vinyl and insulated windows, make a "winter garden" a practical and affordable option that can be enjoyed all year-round.

In this chapter, you'll find dozens of examples of conservatories in a variety of sizes, shapes, and price ranges.

A conservatory lends an elegant attitude to a home.

Striking details make this solid conservatory an impressive addition to the main house.

Operable rooflights provide ventilation.

The glass roof is set in from the walls and raised to make the room feel lighter and more spacious.

Solid timber panels at each corner lend weight to the Georgian-style glazing.

The brick kneewall ties the conservatory to the house.

A deeply molded cornice hides the gutters.

Sturdy brass hardware secures the doors.

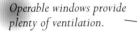 Conservatories are remarkably versatile spaces that can be adapted to many uses.

Operable windows provide plenty of ventilation.

If the sun is too bright, shades can be drawn over the glass ceiling.

Track lighting suspended across the room provides task lighting for the work area.

Designed with a kneewall

to accommodate cabinets, this conservatory houses a sunny kitchen.

The ledge behind the cabinets extends along the room, offering spots for plants and other decorative accessories.

Recessed lights provide ambient light at night and on dreary days.

Here, an artist has created a delightful studio. Fabric panels,

which can be drawn to filter the light when necessary, hang from the ceiling. On a solid wall, shelves and hooks hold props and completed works, while supplies wait in a large chest of drawers.

*Design*Wise

Mark D. Barocco
President,
Renaissance
Conservatories
Leola, PA

• *Plan, Plan, Plan.* If you are like most people, you will build only one conservatory in your lifetime. When conceived, designed and executed properly, a well appointed conservatory can likely become the most favored room in your home. Take time to do your research, and be sure to hire a competent general contractor.

• *Keep it consistent.* A conservatory's unique stand-alone appearance can be a charming addition, provided it has complementary architectural features that are appropriately sympathetic to your home's style. While a period conservatory can add a bit of "instant history," mating a whimsically ornate Victorian conservatory to a formal Georgian Colonial might not garner the kind of attention you are seeking.

• *Watch that sun!* A glass roof can be enticing, but if your site will receive a lot of midday or afternoon sunlight, the amount and type of glass will be an important consideration in creating a comfortable

year-round living space. Glass is best used to preserve a view, to add natural light to the core of a space, to create a plant-friendly environment, to add drama, or all of the above. "An all-glass roof does not a conservatory make," and your conservatory should be as livable as it is beautiful to behold.

• *Annex or extension?* A smaller conservatory often works best with the removal of the shared house wall, effectively extending your living space into your conservatory and opening your home to light and to views of the outside. A bump-out conservatory breakfast nook that becomes part of the kitchen beyond is a good example of this approach. As a conservatory grows in size, it may work better as a separate living space. Being able to isolate a pool or spa conservatory enclosure from the rest of your home provides some obvious advantages for controlling humidity and odors.

• Do it yourself? If you are handy and have the time, you may be able to save money by performing your own installation. If you decide to go it alone, be advised that conservatories often involve proprietary installation techniques requiring specialized construction skills and attention to detail.

Windows open into the bathroom adjoining the conservatory's lantern.

Beadboard-covered walls topped by a collection of windows open this second-floor bathing space to the lantern of a main-floor conservatory. This unique arrangement gives the bathroom a sense of extra space and dimension, as well as gorgeous views.

Electrical fixtures above tubs, spas, or pools must be rated for such use.

Living plants help purify the air and control moisture in spas and other bathing spaces.

This elegant conservatory

houses an invigorating spa. Ventilation is critical for rooms containing pools or spas. Here, a bank of slightly above-floor-height, operable windows provide fresh air and allow moisture to escape.

Outdoor furnishings stand up to the moisture and warmth of the spa's environment.

Take a striking landscape. Add a conservatory. The result is pure drama.

This combination of wildlife habitat and conservatory is paradise for birds and birding enthusiasts alike. Accessories perch on the window ledge, which can also be used as a front-row seat for the action. Potted plants and flowers blend the structure into the landscape.

An arbor-like structure on the side shades this conservatory during certain parts of the day. Wide French doors open to the landscape, bringing the sounds and fragrances of the outdoors into the room.

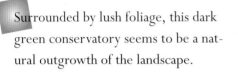 Surrounded by lush foliage, this dark green conservatory seems to be a natural outgrowth of the landscape.

Shaded by large trees and shrubs, these windows don't need protection.

A long crank fits into this lever to open the windows in the ceiling.

The stone ledge at the top of the kneewall provides a cool, water-resistant surface on which to rest potted plants.

Shades filter the sunlight

streaming through the ceiling and
walls of this conservatory and give
its inhabitants some privacy.
When the sun isn't directly
over the conservatory and privacy
isn't an issue, the shades can be
drawn out of the way.

Ivy-covered walls provide a cool backdrop for dining al fresco

in this lean-to conservatory. Especially if located near the kitchen,
conservatories make superb dining spaces.

Conservatories can be designed to fit any situation.

Conservatories are versatile structures that can be tucked into corners, built out from straight walls, or extended from upper stories. Successful designs fit not only the available space, but also the character of the house.

The rectangular shape, hip roof, and stucco knee walls of this conservatory complement the main structure of the house.

Lean-to styles are popular because their simple shapes can be adapted to fit small or unusual spaces. Because they're relatively simple to construct and maintain, lean-to styles often cost less than more complex versions.

Tucked between wings of the house, this conservatory acts much like a breezeway.

This gracious conservatory harmonizes effortlessly with both the house and its surroundings.

Wide French doors can be opened to enjoy the view or the breeze.

The stone patio slopes down and away from the conservatory to direct water away from the structure.

Copper gutters present a distinguished appearance that suits the structure.

The kneewall and step are topped with stone that matches the patio floor.

Wiring for the ceiling fan and wall sconces are hidden inside the framing.

Heat registers are tucked beneath the kneewall ledge.

Inside the conservatory, the mechanicals are cleverly concealed.

*Idea*Wise

If you're adapting unique pieces into plant containers for your conservatory, remember that all planting containers must have drainage. If necessary, drill or punch several ¼" holes (spaced about 4" apart) in the bottom of the container, add a 2" layer of gravel, and fill the remainder of the container with potting soil. To drill holes in ceramic or glass, first use an awl to create a dimple, then drill the hole with a special glass-and-tile bit.

If you need to add a bottom to a container, try shaping hardware cloth to fit the opening. Secure the mesh with a wide bead of silicone caulk, and let it dry. Line the hardware cloth with sphagnum moss, and plant the container as usual.

Splendor in the glass.

Although they're lovely any time of day, proper lighting makes conservatories irresistibly romantic at night.

A lantern glows in the corner.

Simple sconces hold candles on the wall.

Candlelight twinkles on the table.

The warm light of color-correct or pink lightbulbs enhance the effect of lamplight at night.

At night, the glass catches and reflects the light, outlining the framework against the darkness.

Uplights add drama to the palm fronds.

Crystals sparkle from lamps and chandeliers in this elegant room. In a conservatory, all light fixtures should have dimmers so they can be adjusted to suit the occasion and time of day.

Reflected in every pane of glass, candlelight illuminates the night.

Lighting the landscape beyond the conservatory improves the view from both inside and out. Here, stakes hold candles above a charming perennial garden.

Resource Guide

A listing of resources for information, designs, and products found in *IdeaWise Porches & Sunrooms*.

Introduction

page 8
Sunroom by
Amdega
800-449-7348
Freephone 0800 591523
www.amdega.com

page 9
Solarium by
Four Seasons Solar Products
800-FOUR SEASONS
www.FourSeasonsSunrooms.com

page 10 (top)
Home designed by
Lindal Cedar Homes, Inc.
Seattle, Washington
888-4LINDAL
www.lindal.com

page 11 (top)
Home designed by
Lindal Cedar Homes, Inc.
Seattle, Washington
888-4LINDAL
www.lindal.com

page 11 (center, bottom)
Sunrooms by
Four Seasons Solar Products
800-FOUR SEASONS
www.FourSeasonsSunrooms.com

page 12 (top)
Solarium by
Four Seasons Solar Products
800-FOUR SEASONS
www.FourSeasonsSunrooms.com

page 12 (bottom)
Conservatory by
Gorell Grand Additions which offers three lines of sunrooms, including its American Conservatory Series
888-822-2485
www.grandadditions.com

Open Porches

Resource Guide
(continued)

Enclosed Porches

page 58
screened porch by
Marty Graff Custom Homes and Remodeling
Raleigh, NC
919-233-6712
www.martygraff.com

pages 60-61
Screened porch by
Archadeck
Richmond, VA
800-722-4668
www.archadeck.com

pages 66-67 (all)
Screened porches by
Archadeck
Richmond, VA
800-722-4668
www.archadeck.com

page 67 (bottom)
Robert Gerloff, AIA
Robert Gerloff Residential Architects
Minneapolis, MN

pages 68-70 (all)
porches and deck by
DeckWright, LLC
Atlanta, Georgia
770-455-7712
www.deckwright.com

page 74
enclosed porch by
Stuart M. Jones Custom Homes, Inc.
Raleigh, NC
919-782-5651
www.stuartjonescustomhomes.com

page 75 (both)
porch and sunroom by
Archadeck
Richmond, VA
800-722-4668
www.archadeck.com

Sunrooms

Resource Guide

(continued)

Solariums

page 100
Solarium by
Four Seasons Solar Products
800-FOUR SEASONS
www.FourSeasonsSunrooms.com

page 102-103 (top)
Solariums by
Four Seasons Solar Products
800-FOUR SEASONS
www.FourSeasonsSunrooms.com

page 103 (bottom)
solarium by
Buena Vista Sunrooms
800-747-3324
www.sunroom.com

page 104 (top)
solarium by
Buena Vista Sunrooms
800-747-3324
www.sunroom.com

pages 104 (bottom)-105
solariums by
Four Seasons Solar Products
800-FOUR SEASONS
www.FourSeasonsSunrooms.com

pages 106-107
solariums by
Four Seasons Solar Products
800-FOUR SEASONS
www.FourSeasonsSunrooms.com

pages 108-109 (bottom)
solarium by
Buena Vista Sunrooms
800-747-3324
www.sunroom.com

page 109 (top)
solariums by
Four Seasons Solar Products
800-FOUR SEASONS
www.FourSeasonsSunrooms.com

page 110
solariums by
Four Seasons Solar Products
800-FOUR SEASONS
www.FourSeasonsSunrooms.com

page 111
solarium by
Buena Vista Sunrooms
800-747-3324
www.sunroom.com

page 112
Design Wise tips by
Al Meffan
Patio Enclosures, Inc.
Macedonia, OH

page 113 (both)
solariums by
Four Seasons Solar Products
800-FOUR SEASONS
www.FourSeasonsSunrooms.com

Conservatories

Photo Credits

Front cover photo and title page: Photo courtesy of Amdega, Ltd.

Back cover: (top left) Photo courtesy of Renaissance Conservatories; (top right) ©Beth Connant/Acclaim Images; (center and bottom left) ©DeckWright, LLC in Atlanta, Georgia; (bottom right) photo courtesy of Four Seasons Sunrooms.

p. 2 (top): Photo courtesy of Lindal Cedar Homes, Seattle, Washington.

p. 3: (bottom left) Photo courtesy of Amdega, Ltd; (bottom right) ©Brand X Pictures.

p. 4: ©Fritz Von Der Schulenburg/The Interior Archive.

p. 6: ©Fritz Von Der Schulenburg/The Interior Archive.

p. 7: ©Beth Connant/Acclaim Images.

p. 8: Photo courtesy of Amdega, Ltd.

p. 9: Photo courtesy of Four Seasons Sunrooms.

p. 10: (top) Photo courtesy of Lindal Cedar Homes, Seattle, Washington; (bottom) ©Fritz Von Der Schulenburg/The Interior Archive.

p. 11: (top and bottom) Photo courtesy of Lindal Cedar Homes, Seattle, Washington; (center) Photo courtesy of Four Seasons Sunrooms.

p. 12: (top)Photo courtesy of Four Seasons Sunrooms; (bottom) Photo courtesy of Gorell Grand Additions/American Conservatory Series.

p. 14: Photo courtesy of Lindal Cedar Homes, Seattle, Washington.

pp. 16-17: ©Gay Bumgarnar/Alamy.

pp. 18-19: (both) ©Thomas Halstein/www.outsight.com.

p. 20: ©Steve Sloan/quaintimages.com.

p. 21: ©Royalty-free/Corbis.

p. 22: (top) ©Royalty-free/Corbis; (bottom) ©Brand X Pictures.

p. 23: Photo courtesy of Lindal Cedar Homes, Seattle, Washington.

pp. 24-25 ©Steve Sloan/quaintimages.com.

p. 26: (top) ©Royalty-free/Corbis.

p. 27 (top) ©Steve Sloan/quaintimages.com; (bottom) ©Royalty-free/Corbis.

pp. 28-29: (top) Image ©Royce Bair/Acclaim Images; (bottom) ©Royalty-free/Corbis.

p. 30: (top) ©Royalty-free/Corbis; (bottom) ©Steve Sloan/quaintimages.com.

p. 31: ©Steve Sloan/quaintimages.com.

pp. 32-33: (both) ©Gay Bumgarnar/Alamy.

pp. 34-35: (both) ©Royalty-free/Corbis.

p. 36: ©Simon Upton/The Interior Archive.

p. 37: ©Fritz Von Der Schulenburg/The Interior Archive.

p. 39: ©Fritz Von Der Schulenburg/The Interior Archive.

pp. 40-41: (all) ©DeckWright, LLC in Atlanta, Georgia.

pp.42-43: (both) ©Fritz Von Der Schulenburg/The Interior Archive.

p. 44: Photo by Robert C. Lautman/courtesy of Anthony Wilder Design/Build, Inc.

p. 45: Photo courtesy of Lindal Cedar Homes, Seattle, Washington.

p. 46: ©Fritz Von Der Schulenburg/The Interior Archive.

p. 47: ©Ray Strawbridge Photo/www.strawbridgephoto.com for Bost Custom Homes.

p. 48: ©Thomas Halstein/www.outsight.com.

p. 49: ©Steve Sloan/quaintimages.com.

pp. 50-51: (all) ©Steve Sloan/quaintimages.com.

p. 52: ©Steve Sloan/quaintimages.com.

p. 53: ©Royalty-free/Corbis.

p. 54: ©Steve Sloan/quaintimages.com.

p. 55: Beateworks, Inc./Alamy.

p. 56: ©Steve Sloan/quaintimages.com.

p.57: ©Thomas Halstein/www.outsight.com.

p. 58: ©Ray Strawbridge Photo/www.strawbridgephoto.com for Marty Graff Custom Homes and Remodeling.

pp. 60-61: Photo courtesy of Archadeck.

p.61: ©David Carmack Photography, Boston for Feinmann Remodeling, Inc.

p. 62: ©Fritz Von Der Schulenburg/The Interior Archive.

p. 63: ©Fritz Von Der Schulenburg/The Interior Archive.

p. 64: ©Fritz Von Der Schulenburg/The Interior Archive.

p. 65: ©David Livingston/davidduncunlivingston.com.

pp. 66-67: (all) Photos courtesy of Archadeck.

pp. 68-70: (all) ©DeckWright, LLC in Atlanta, Georgia.

p. 71:(both) ©David Livingston/davidduncunlivingston.com.

pp. 72-73: (both) ©Fritz Von Der Schulenburg/The Interior Archive.

p.74: ©Ray Strawbridge Photo/ www.strawbridgephoto.com for Stuart M. Jones Custom Homes, Inc.

p.75: (both) Photos courtesy of Archadeck.

p. 76: ©Fritz Von Der Schulenburg/The Interior Archive.

p.78-79: (both) Photos courtesy of Lindal Cedar Homes, Seattle, Washington.

pp. 80-81: ©David Livingston/ davidduncunlivingston.com.

p.82: (top, bottom) Photos courtesy of Lindal Cedar Homes, Seattle, Washington; (center) Photo courtesy of Four Seasons Sunrooms.

p. 83: Photo courtesy of Lindal Cedar Homes, Seattle, Washington.

p. 84: (top) Photo courtesy of Four Seasons Sunrooms, (bottom) Photo courtesy of Lindal Cedar Homes, Seattle, Washington.

p. 85: Photo courtesy of Four Seasons Sunrooms.

p. 86: Photo courtesy of Lindal Cedar Homes, Seattle, Washington.

p. 87: Photo courtesy of Four Seasons Sunrooms.

pp. 88-89: Photo courtesy of Lindal Cedar Homes, Seattle, Washington.

p. 90: Photo courtesy of Lindal Cedar Homes, Seattle, Washington.

p. 91: ©David Livingston/davidduncunlivingston.com.

p. 92: (top) Photo courtesy of Lindal Cedar Homes, Seattle, Washington; (bottom) Elizabeth Whitting & Associates/Alamy.

p.93: Photo courtesy of Lindal Cedar Homes, Seattle, Washington.

p. 94: ©Fritz Von Der Schulenburg/The Interior Archive.

p.95: Photo courtesy of Lindal Cedar Homes, Seattle, Washington.

p. 96: (both)© David Livingston/ davidduncunlivingston.com.

p. 98: ©Fritz Von Der Schulenburg/The Interior Archive.

p. 99: ©Ellizabeth Whitting & Associates/Alamy; (bottom) ©Fritz Von Der Schulenburg/The Interior Archive.

p. 100: Photo courtesy of Four Seasons Sunrooms.

p.102: Photo courtesy of Four Seasons Sunrooms.

p. 103: (top) Photo courtesy of Four Seasons Sunrooms, (bottom) Photo courtesy of Buena Vista Sunrooms.

p. 104: (top) Photo courtesy of Buena Vista Sunrooms;

(bottom) Photo courtesy of Four Seasons Sunrooms.

p. 105: Photo courtesy of Four Seasons Sunrooms.

pp. 106-107: (all) Photos courtesy of Four Seasons Sunrooms.

p.108: Photo courtesy of Buena Vista Sunrooms.

p. 109: (top) Photo courtesy of Four Seasons Sunrooms; (bottom) Photo courtesy of Buena Vista Sunrooms.

p. 110: Photo courtesy of Four Seasons Sunrooms.

p. 111: Photo courtesy of Buena Vista Sunrooms.

p. 113: (both) Photo courtesy of Four Seasons Sunrooms.

p. 114: Photo courtesy of Amdega, Ltd.

pp. 116-117: Photo courtesy of Amdega, Ltd.

p. 118 (top): Photo courtesy of Renaissance Conservatories; (bottom) ©Fritz Von Der Schulenburg/The Interior Archive.

pp.120-121: (all) Photos courtesy of Renaissance Conservatories.

p. 122: Photo courtesy of Amdega, Ltd.

p. 123: (top) Photo by Robert C. Lautman/courtesy of Anthony Wilder Design/Build, Inc.; (bottom) Photo courtesy of Amdega, Ltd.

p. 124: Photo courtesy of Amdega, Ltd.

p. 125: ©Fritz Von Der Schulenburg/The Interior Archive.

p. 126: ©Fritz Von Der Schulenburg/The Interior Archive.

p. 127: (top) Photo courtesy of Gorell Grand Additions/ American Conservatory Series; (bottom) ©Fritz Von Der Schulenburg/The Interior Archive.

pp. 128-129: Photos courtesy of Renaissance Conservatories.

pp. 130-131: Photos courtesy of Amdega, Ltd.

p. 132: (top) Photo courtesy of Renaissance Conservatories; (bottom) Photo courtesy of Amdega, Ltd.

p. 133: Photo courtesy of Amdega, Ltd.

p. 134: Photo courtesy of Lindal Cedar Homes, Seattle, Washington.

p. 135: ©Steve Sloan/quaintimages.com.

p. 136: © DeckWright, LLC in Atlanta, Georgia.

p. 137: Photo courtesy of Lindal Cedar Homes, Seattle, Washington.

p. 138: Photo courtesy of Four Seasons Sunrooms.

p. 139: Photo courtesy of Amdega, Ltd.

Index

CREATIVE PUBLISHING INTERNATIONAL

Complete Guide to Bathrooms
Complete Guide to Building Decks
Complete Guide to Ceramic & Stone Tile
Complete Guide to Creative Landscapes
Complete Guide to Easy Woodworking Projects
Complete Guide to Finishing Touches
   for Yards & Gardens
Complete Guide to Flooring
Complete Guide to Home Carpentry
Complete Guide to Home Masonry
Complete Guide to Home Plumbing
Complete Guide to Home Storage
Complete Guide to Home Wiring
Complete Guide to Kitchens
Complete Guide to Outdoor Wood Projects
Complete Guide to Painting & Decorating
Complete Guide to Roofing & Siding
Complete Guide to Windows & Doors
Complete Photo Guide to Home Repair
Complete Photo Guide to Home Improvement
Complete Photo Guide to Outdoor Home Repair

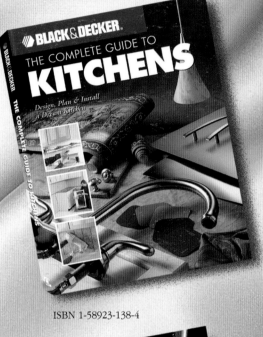

ISBN 1-58923-138-4

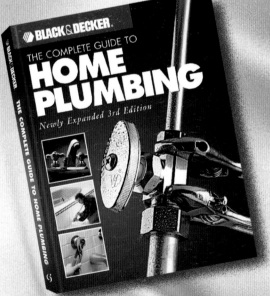

ISBN 0-86573-428-3

CREATIVE PUBLISHING INTERNATIONAL
18705 LAKE DRIVE EAST
CHANHASSEN, MN 55317

WWW.CREATIVEPUB.COM